Dear Gra[   ]y

I hope you
this book
the time u
in Manchester - as well as future
visits to come!

All my love and fondest of regards,
Martha
x x x x

MANCHESTER
THE GREAT CITY

Mike Heath

HALSGROVE

First published in Great Britain in 2016

Copyright © Mike Heath 2016

British Library Cataloguing-in-Publication Data
A CIP record for this title is available from the British Library

ISBN 978 0 85704 294 1

HALSGROVE
Halsgrove House,
Ryelands Business Park,
Bagley Road, Wellington, Somerset TA21 9PZ
Tel: 01823 653777   Fax: 01823 216796
email: sales@halsgrove.com

Part of the Halsgrove group of companies.
Information on all Halsgrove titles is available at: www.halsgrove.com

Printed in China by Everbest Printing Investment Ltd

MANCHESTER'S 'COAT OF ARMS' AND THE 'BUSY BEE'

The city's coat of arms was granted in 1842 and is a classic heraldic design. On it a shield bears the image of a ship, supported by an antelope and lion on either side. The shield is crowned by a globe covered in bees.

The ship in full sail pays homage to the city's growing trade and enterprise. The lion is a symbol of strength, while the antelope, which is actually a mythical beast, means peace and harmony, extreme courage and discipline. The city's motto at the foot of the piece, *Concilio et Labore* translates to 'by council and work'.

The globe covered in bees is a symbol of industriousness, the bees becoming a symbol for the city appearing all over Manchester on bollards, planters and litter bins in addition to many of the city's historic buildings.

INTRODUCTION

Whilst Manchester can trace its roots back to Roman times, it was the Industrial Revolution that saw it spring to the forefront of world attention primarily as a result of its leading role in world manufacture and production of textiles. Leaders of commerce, science and technology helped to create a vibrant economy and much of the nation's wealth in Victorian times was created in this region.

Mills were built to house the looms that were initially water-powered until the Duke of Bridgewater brought his coal into the town via the first true canal (1761). The workers and their families needed homes to live in and food to live on. Hence the building of basic housing terraces and tenements alongside markets where fresh meat, fish and vegetables could be purchased.

The quest to speed up transport saw the very first passenger railway line, that between Liverpool and Manchester, constructed. This terminated at the very first passenger station located at Liverpool Road (1830).

Corn distribution was added to the town's trade portfolio by which time the town had grown to such an extent that City status was bestowed in 1853, six years after the church of St Mary had become a cathedral.

This frantic industrial activity caused an explosion in the population which rapidly increased from 75,000 in 1801 to 142,000 thirty years later. The city's infrastructure struggled to cope and many people had to live in dreadful slums. Slowly improvements were made. In 1816 a water company began to pipe water through iron pipes to those that could afford it. Street lighting started to appear from the 1820s.

The nation's banks began to establish themselves and local government moved into in a new Town Hall (1876). Shopping malls emerged, national papers were printed locally, the first public library was opened and Manchester University was founded (1903).

Without a coastline of its own and to by-pass the taxes levied by Liverpool's Dock and Railway Companies, the city developed trade with the outside world with the construction of the Manchester Ship Canal and Manchester Docks (1894). The world's first industrial estate, Trafford Park, was developed alongside on land once owned by the Trafford family.

The first half of the twentieth century saw the council start to demolish the slums and replace them with the first council housing and there was the emergence of new industries such as flour milling, biscuits and breakfast cereal manufacture. Elsewhere the textile trade had already started to decline, a problem exacerbated by the Second World War. In the aftermath the city had to not only rebuild the areas destroyed by the conflict but also deal with the decline in the industries that had brought it to prominence. The sixties heralded 'skyscraper' construction across the city with most notably the CIS Tower and Piccadilly Plaza developments reaching for the sky.

The seventies saw the dilapidated warehouses around Charlotte Street given a new lease of life as a new 'Chinatown' developed, its place in history cemented with the arrival of the first true Chinese Imperial arch to be erected in Europe. Elsewhere the UK's largest inner-city shopping mall the Arndale Centre was opened.

Tourism was becoming an industry in its own right. In 1969, the city had opened a Museum of Science and Technology followed ten years later by a Museum of Transport adding to the ancient buildings, historic libraries and galleries already attracting visitors. In 1982 Castlefield became the first area in the United Kingdom to be given Urban Heritage Park status.

The late eighties and early nineties saw attitudes moderate, allowing the gay and transgender community to come out of the dark shadows of the mills along Canal Street and create what has become the 'Gay Village', one of the most flamboyant nightlife destinations in the city. Inner city transport was enhanced when trams returned to the streets as the Manchester Metrolink opened, the first modern street running rail system in the United Kingdom.

In 1996 a bomb planted in a lorry and parked by the IRA alongside the Arndale Centre caused devastation with shops and offices, within a half-mile radius, destroyed. This atrocity did not break the spirit of the city; in fact it gave greater impetus to its regeneration. Renovated Victorian complexes like the Printworks and The Corn Exchange became popular retail and entertainment centres, the Arndale Centre was greatly improved and all over the city modern architecture has created buildings from concrete, steel and glass to stand shoulder to shoulder with monuments from the industrial past.

Manchester has become Britain's most important city outside London.

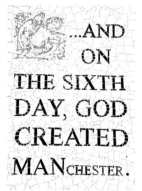

...AND ON THE SIXTH DAY, GOD CREATED MANCHESTER.

A Mark Kennedy mosaic on the wall at Afflecks.

CASTLEFIELD

Being the site of the first recorded human settlement in the city, the location of the first industrial canal and the destination for the first railway passengers, Castlefield was given Urban Heritage Park status in 1982, the first in the United Kingdom. Once the hub of the Industrial Revolution, the area is now one of the most tranquil in Manchester with canal-side bars and restaurants amongst former warehouses that have been converted into popular apartments. On the canal itself flower-decked narrowboats, now leisure crafts, are moored beneath the railway viaducts over which the trains and trams clatter their way to and from the city centre.

CASTLEFIELD – ROMAN FORT

The earliest definite record of a settlement in Manchester came when the Romans marched into the north-west of England in AD79 and set up camp here, constructing a timber fort called Mamucium. By the time they left, around AD410, the fort had been enlarged and rebuilt in stone and the village that had been set up nearby had fallen into disrepair. Much of what remained of the castle was destroyed during the construction of the canals and railways. However, as part of the area's regeneration, remains, which include the fort's gatehouse, were re-built on exposed foundations and are now on open display to the public.

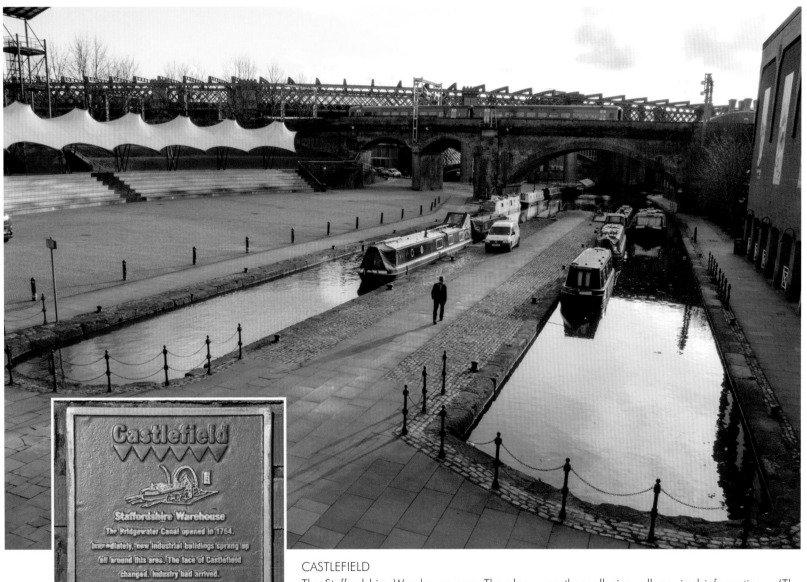

Castlefield
ˇˇˇˇ

Staffordshire Warehouse
The Bridgewater Canal opened in 1764.
Immediately, new industrial buildings sprang up
all around this area. The face of Castlefield
changed. Industry had arrived.

The two arms of canal, shaped like a tuning fork,
allowed two barges at a time to enter the
Staffordshire Warehouse to load and unload.
It was one of Castlefield's first warehouses, and
around this huge building were sheds, offices
and other warehouses.

CASTLEFIELD

The Staffordshire Warehouse arm. The plaque on the wall gives all required information – 'The Bridgewater Canal opened in 1764. Immediately, new industrial buildings sprang up all around this area. The face of Castlefield changed. Industry had arrived. The two arms of canal, shaped like a tuning fork, allowed two barges at a time to enter the Staffordshire Warehouse to load and unload. It was one of Castlefield's first warehouses and around this huge building were sheds, offices and other warehouses.' With the warehouses gone, the natural amphitheatre remains and was developed to create an events arena for live music and outdoor theatre performances.

Victorian engineering. From left to right, the southern red brick viaduct with the cast iron arch bridge was constructed in 1849 for the Manchester, South Junction and Altrincham Railway. The central high level iron truss girder viaduct, known as the Cornbrook Viaduct dates from 1877 when built by the Midland Railway Company for the Cheshire Lines Committee. The third, northern, viaduct was completed in 1894. This high level tubular-steel-supported viaduct, decorated with turrets, gave the Great Northern Railway access to their warehouses in Deansgate. These closed in 1963.

Built in 1996 the Merchant's Bridge spans the basin on a sweeping curve. This footbridge is wider at the centre than at each end to allow pedestrians to stop and admire the view without delaying those with less time on their hands. On the right is the oldest surviving warehouse on the canal basin, the Merchant's Warehouse, which dates from the 1820s. Note the pair of large shipping holes which gave access to bays allowing the loading and unloading of barges within the building.

Having escaped demolition and despite being badly damaged by fire in the 1970s the warehouse was completely refurbished between 1995 and 1997 and it now provides prestigious waterfront office accommodation.

Below: Having been disused for many years, the condition of the Cornbrook and Great Northern Railway Viaducts was reviewed when a route for the Altrincham branch of the Metrolink was sought. The Cornbrook Viaduct was found to be in better condition and was refurbished 1990-91. The line to Altrincham opened the following year.

Left: It is not only the vacated warehouses that have provided space for the new bars and restaurants. As in many other locations around the city, the arches beneath the railway have been transformed to create trendy canal-side establishments.

At the far end of the basin is another 'new' footbridge. The Grocer's Footbridge, erected in 1990, is adjacent to the site of the Grocers Warehouse that was one of the first large warehouses built on the basin. In 1811 it was sold to the Manchester Grocers Company (hence the name) and from here vessels sailed daily to and from the company's wharf in Liverpool. The original warehouse was demolished in 1960 but a partial reconstruction, out of view to the left of the chapel, was carried out in 1987.

The Congregational Chapel, which itself dates from 1858, has had a very interesting recent history. In the 1980s Pete Waterman converted it into a recording studio and for a while many of the popular music hits recorded under the Stock, Aitken and Waterman banner were recorded here. It has since been redeveloped into offices.

MUSEUM OF SCIENCE & INDUSTRY

Unusually for a museum, here it is the buildings themselves that have a more significant historic importance than the exhibits housed within. The Liverpool Road Station and adjacent warehouse date from 1830 when they became the terminus for the very first passenger railway line linking Liverpool and Manchester.

Right: The museum currently has two working steam locomotives.

Agecroft No.1 is an 0-4-0 saddletank that worked at the Agecroft Power Station on the outskirts of the city.

'Planet' is a museum-built (1992) replica of a locomotive that was constructed in 1830 for use on the Liverpool to Manchester route.

Over the years the museum has been able to receive visiting locomotives via a connection to the main network. Unfortunately this link has been severed as part of Network Rail's 'Ordsall Link' development linking Manchester's Victoria and Piccadilly Stations. Thus 180 years after the first ever passenger train arrived, the station will never again receive steam loco-motives from the main-line!!

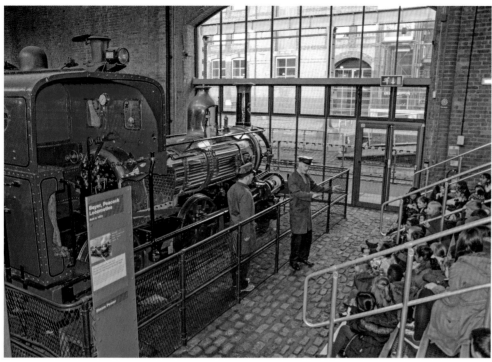

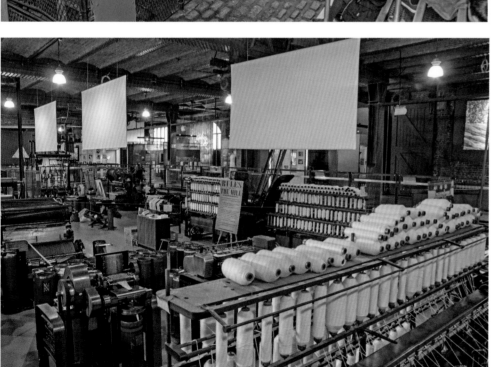

The museum's range of exhibits is vast, reflecting Manchester's industrial history and development. The workings of steam locomotives and textile machinery are regularly demonstrated and other exhibitions covering gas, water, electricity, computers, photography, space and aviation are equally impressive.

The air and space exhibits have their own building across the road from the MOSI entrance. This impressive structure was built by Mangnall & Littlewood in 1876 to house the open-air Lower Campsfield Market. In the early 1900s the building became the City Exhibition Hall and during the Second World War was used for the manufacture of barrage balloons. It has carried out its current role since 1983. The skeletal steel frame with its extensive glazing has created a well-lit open exhibition area that houses a splendid array of aeroplanes that includes a Shackleton Bomber and a Japanese suicide bomber. Manchester's motor vehicle history is also represented with an early Rolls-Royce assembled at the company's first factory in nearby Hulme

ST JOHN'S STREET

Built alongside St John's Gardens, once the site of a Georgian church, this is the sole surviving Georgian terrace in Central Manchester. The handsome houses on the street were built piecemeal, as required, in the late eighteenth and early nineteenth centuries meaning that they are not identical. Most are now offices or consulting rooms.

CORONATION STREET

Probably the most famous fictional street in the United Kingdom. First broadcast by ITV in December 1960, *Coronation Street* remains one of the most popular television programmes in Britain. The back story is that it was based around a street in the fictional town of Weatherfield that was built in the early 1900s and named to celebrate the coronation of King Edward VII. it was produced at the Granada Television Studios, on the edge of Castlefield, until 2014 when the company moved to Media City. (All photos Darren Heath.)

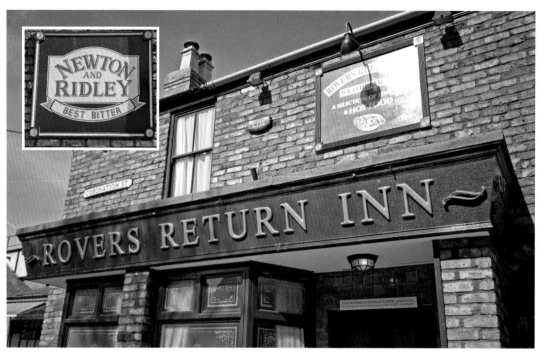

From the sixties the 'set' developed with the programme but it was not until the 1980s that the permanent full street set was built. Further development included factories, a builder's yard and in 2008 a block of luxury flats, Victoria Court. When the site was vacated by Granada the purchasing developers saw an opportunity to open the set to the public for a period before site redevelopment commenced. Thousands flocked to the cobbled street to walk past the terraced houses, café, corner shop, newsagents, butchers, chippy, textile factory and of course the local pub the 'Rovers Return'. (All photos Darren Heath.)

ROCHDALE CANAL   When opened in 1804 this 33-mile-long waterway that links the Castlefield basin in Manchester with the Calder and Hebble navigation at Sowerby Bridge was the first trans-Pennine canal route. It was used to transport coal, agricultural produce and materials for the textile industry between the two counties. The last boat crossed the Pennines in 1937 and with the exception of the section through Manchester, the canal fell into disrepair. Progressive reclamation work that started in the seventies saw the entire route once again navigable in 2002.

Above: There are a total of 92 locks on the canal with No. 92 connecting with the Bridgewater Canal at Castlefield. When the Rochdale Canal first opened the Duke of Bridgewater was reluctant to allow a connection to his waterway so it terminated at a basin near Dale Street, Piccadilly. Once convinced of the benefits the Duke allowed the extension through the city to Castlefield which involved the construction of nine locks. His only condition was that his own workforce constructed the last lock connecting with his own waterway. Thus lock 92 has always been referred to as the Duke's lock. The lock keeper's cottage is now in private ownership and thought to be the only detached residential property in the city centre.

Left: The section between locks 92 and 91, at Deansgate, ran through a shallow tunnel when first constructed, but this was soon opened out. Now it passes beneath an impressive skewed bridge constructed as part of the Manchester, South Junction and Altrincham Railway's brick viaduct referred to earlier.

PETER'S FIELD

This area is the Conference Quarter of the city.

Left: The section between locks 91 and 90 is known as Deansgate Locks, the canal passing beneath Deansgate just behind the lock keeper's cottage seen at the far end of the photograph. The ten railway arches that line this section, running parallel with Whitworth Street West, have been converted to six contemporary bars and a Comedy Club. It is a very popular meeting place in the summer with its terrace drinking/eating areas. The Deansgate Metrolink station is handy, being immediately above the arches.

Below, left and right: The section of canal around lock 89 has seen much residential development, including homes for our feathered friends. Here there is a small branch that is a remnant of the former Manchester and Salford Junction Canal that linked with Water Street, near the River Irwell.

21

BRIDGEWATER HALL

Alongside this small branch of the canal is the state-of-the-art concert venue – the Bridgewater Hall. Opened by Her Majesty the Queen in December 1996, this internationally renowned hall must be one of the most acoustically insulated buildings in the world. Not only is it constructed from solid reinforced concrete that is moulded and cast like a giant sculpture, but the whole structure 'floats' on almost 300 earthquake-proof giant springs which means that there is no rigid connection between the building and its foundations. It is thus completely insulated against sound and vibration from outside.

The Hall is home to three resident orchestras and hosts over 250 performances each year covering the world of classical music, rock, pop, jazz and much, much more.

THE MANCHESTER CENTRAL CONVENTION COMPLEX

Formerly known as Gmex, this is an exhibition and conference centre housed in what was the Manchester Central railway station built for the Cheshire Lines Committee between 1875 and 1880. The single span wrought iron truss structure is 550 feet long, spans 220 feet and is 90 feet high at its apex. The station had six platforms and was shared by the Midland Railway Company who ran express services to and from London's St Pancras Station. Closed in 1969 the building fell into disrepair until purchased by the Greater Manchester Council in 1982. Work to convert it to an exhibition hall commenced immediately and it opened in 1986. The station's vast undercroft is now a car park for the Bridgewater Hall.

Above and opposite: THE MIDLAND HOTEL

Across from the Central Station the Midland Railway built one of the most eye-catching buildings in the city perhaps to match the impressive St Pancras Station Hotel at its London terminus. Completed in 1903 the building is clad in combinations of red brick, polished granite and pink and brown terracotta.

In 1904 the first meeting between Henry Royce and Charles Stewart Rolls took place in the hotel. Royce had already developed and driven cars in the North West and Rolls, who owned a car sales business in London, had set the world land speed record of 93mph in 1903. At the meeting Rolls agreed to become the sole distributor of Royce's cars and two years later the new Rolls-Royce Company was formed. The historic meeting is commemorated with a plaque in the main entrance hall.

THE PEVERIL OF THE PEAK

Just along Great Bridgewater Street is one of central Manchester's last surviving pre-twentieth century pubs. This simple two-storey Victorian building was remodelled in 1900 and given the striking lime-green glazed tile exterior. Internally modernisation has thankfully been resisted and the beautiful timber panelled bar and screens complete with coloured glass panels have been retained. As well as the drinks on offer punters are attracted to what is said to be the oldest continuously used table football table in the country. Who could ask for more?

(The derivation of the unusual name has two possibilities. It is the title of an 1822 novel by Walter Scott and is also the name used by one of the best known stagecoaches that travelled between Manchester and London.)

THE PALACE THEATRE

The Rochdale Canal now passes beneath Oxford Street on which stands one of Manchester's principal theatres, the Palace Theatre. This was designed by Alfred Darbyshire and opened as the Palace of Varieties in May 1891. At the time the entertainment put on by this music hall met with much opposition from the local Methodists. The decline of the music halls following the Great War saw the 'Palace' turn to more conventional performances with dramas, Christmas pantomimes and shows by the popular entertainers of the day. Closure in the 1970s was averted and the building was refurbished, reopening in 1981, since when it has put on a variety of shows that have kept the auditorium filled.

The building's unflattering beige tile cladding was added in 1956 but internally the building retains the splendid auditorium which is well worth viewing whatever the show.

THE PALACE HOTEL Also standing on Oxford Street is the imposing Palace Hotel, formerly the Refuge Assurance Company's headquarters. It was built in three phases between 1891 and 1932. The original corner building was extended 1910-12 and included the clock tower which has become one of Manchester's best known landmarks. The original corner entrance (now blanked off) features a terracotta castle at the top of the ornate surround. This symbolised security for those trusting their money with Refuge Assurance – present day bankers take note!

The building's interior is as lavish as the exterior, with its richly glazed tile work, plasterwork and panelling and its marvellous marble and bronze staircase. The Refuge Assurance Company moved into Cheshire in 1989 and the building's conversion to a 252-bedroom hotel commenced two years later.

MANCHESTER UNIVERSITY The University of Manchester was founded in 1851, thanks to the legacy of a local industrialist, John Owens. By 1870 Owens College had grown to need new premises and in 1873 the John Owens building was completed on Oxford Road, south of the city centre. This was just one of a number of buildings of what is known as the Old Quadrangle which were completed in 1903. In 1880 the college was one of a number that combined to form England's first civic university, the federal Victoria University. In 1900 the constituent colleges separated and in 1903 Owens College was reconstituted as the Victoria University of Manchester. Whilst often referred to as the 'University of Manchester' it was not until the merger with the University of Manchester Institute of Science and Technology (UMIST) in 2004 that this became its official title.

The Whitworth Hall building was completed in 1902 and is named in honour of Sir Joseph Whitworth, a Mancunian industrialist who bequeathed much of his amassed fortune to fund many public developments in the city. The Hall is used for all the university's Graduation Ceremonies where the successes continue to be celebrated in the traditional manner.

THE GAY VILLAGE

The now pedestrianised Canal Street, on the west bank of the Rochdale Canal was as recently as the 1980s a little-known run-down area with a red light district reputation at a time of gay suppression and repression. However since the early 1990s the progressive opening of new swish bars and smart restaurants have seen this once dark and dismal area develop into what is now marketed the 'World Famous Canal Street', a bustling quarter dedicated to gay, lesbian, bisexual and transgender culture and is also the venue for the UK's most successful Annual Pride event.

The culmination of the 'Pride' event is a firework display and a very moving candlelit vigil in the adjacent Sackville Gardens when hundreds of candles are lit in memory of people that have lost their battle against HIV and AIDS, as well as acknowledging the continuing fight against the epidemic.

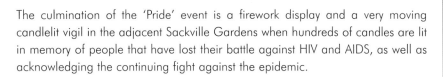

Sackville Gardens, originally known as Whitworth Gardens, is described by the council as 'a green resource for city centre workers, local residents and visitors'. In addition to the 'Beacon of Hope' column and 'Transgender Memorial' (far left and left) at the centre of the gardens is this life-size statue. It is of mathematician Alan Turing who worked at Bletchley Park during the Second World War where he helped the code breakers decipher German naval codes and with the now famous uncovering of the settings for the Enigma machine. In 1948 he was at Manchester University working on the Manchester Mark 1, one of the world's earliest true computers. Notwithstanding his outstanding war record and academic achievements he was subsequently arrested and prosecuted for his homosexuality. His exemplary career was over and in 1954 he committed suicide. Posthumously he has received the recognition he deserved with a Manchester road, bridge and building now bearing his name.

This statue, positioned in 2001, shows Turing holding an apple. He is said to have committed suicide by lacing an apple with cyanide.

SACKVILLE BUILDING (UMIST)

Just across Whitworth Street from the gardens is this magnificent building, by Spalding & Cross, which has been home to the study of science, technology and engineering for over 100 years. It was opened in 1902 for the Manchester Municipal Technical School which received independent university status in 1956. From 1966 it became known as the University of Manchester Institute of Science and Technology, colloquially UMIST and in 2004 it united with the Victoria University of Manchester (see earlier) to form the University of Manchester.

VIMTO GARDENS

On the southern side of the Sackville Building is Granby Row. It is here, in a small terraced house, that in 1908, during the heyday of temperance bars, a herbalist called Noel Nicholls created his unique blend of herbs, spices and fruit essences and made his first barrel of Vimto.

The fruit drink that is most popular in the North of England is actually sold in over 65 countries around the world and whilst the Nicholls family, who manufactured it in various locations around the North West, have long since sold the business to an outside company, they still retain control of its secret recipe.

This historic place in the drink's history is commemorated with an oak sculpture of a giant Vimto bottle surrounded by fruit.

THE TIN BATH

Manchester, with its railway history, is on the route of many steam-hauled railtours. The annual 'The Tin Bath' railtour, which in 2016 was a return trip between Preston – Bolton – Manchester – Sheffield, takes in many secondary lines in East Lancashire and West Yorkshire and usually passes close to Holmfirth, home of the extremely popular long running television comedy *Last of The Summer Wine*. The railtour title honours the memory of Compo's many adventurous trips down a hillside or road in a tin bath!

For those interested, the locomotives hauling this special through Manchester, photographed on the viaduct that links Deansgate with Piccadilly (the Sackville Building in the background), are Black 5 Class No.44871 and LMS 'Jubilee' Class No. 45699 named 'Galatea'.

CHINATOWN

In the late sixties and early seventies, as the textile trade moved away, the old Victorian cotton warehouses around Nicholas Street, George Street and Faulkner Street were becoming redundant. Chinese entrepreneurs began to take over the lower floors opening restaurants to serve the city's business district. The success of these ventures attracted not only more restaurants but also the services required to support them. The area has developed into a vibrant distinct quarter with its own arts centre, restaurants, ethnic grocery stores, medical shops, health facilities, care homes, financial and legal centres. In 1987 the magnificent arch, a gift from Manchester City Council, was erected on Faulkner Street. The arch (known in Mandarin Chinese as 'Paifang') was constructed in China and was the first true Imperial Chinese Arch located in Europe.

(Left: Darren Heath)

The annual Chinese new year celebrations are marked with a dragon-led parade from the Town Hall (Albert) Square to Chinatown. The crowds are entertained with Chinese dancers, music and acrobats. Street stalls offer oriental nourishment and souvenirs and the celebrations culminate in a spectacular firework display.

41

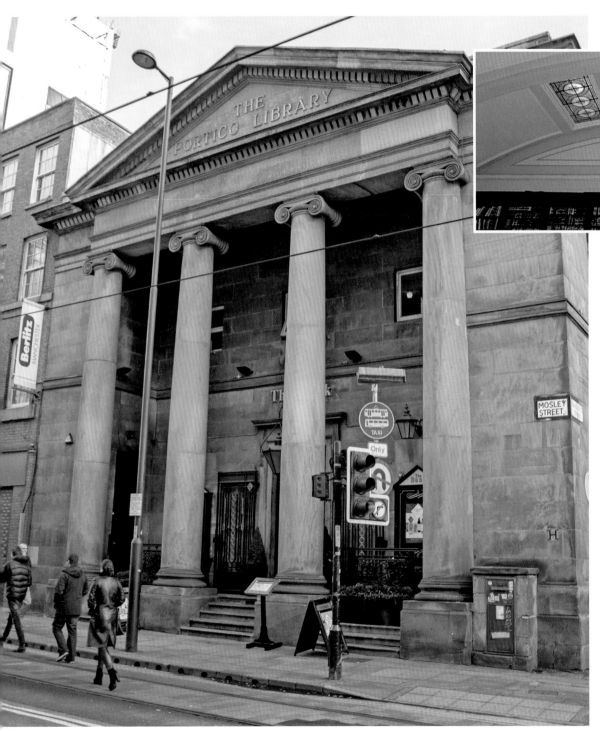

The area that has become Chinatown was first developed in the eighteenth century around the 1786-built church of St James. Several notable institutions were attracted to this location and these included the Scientific and Medical Society which was to become Owens College Medical School (Faulkner Street) and the Literary and Philosophical Society (George Street). This trend continued into the nineteenth century on the surrounding main roads where institutions such as the Portico Library and the Manchester Institution were founded. The latter is now the City Art Gallery. By the end of the nineteenth century commercial pressure brought about the demise of the area and saw the emergence of warehouse construction.

THE PORTICO LIBRARY
The Portico stands at the corner of Mosley Street with Charlotte Street and was built by Thomas Harrison 1802-6. Borne out of a desire of local businessmen to establish an 'institute uniting the advantages of a newsroom and a library' and funded through member's subscriptions the library opened in 1806. Whilst it now just occupies the upper floor, accessed off Charlotte Street, it continues to fulfil the founder's original ambitions and the beauty of its interior has been retained, virtually unchanged since the early nineteenth century.

The blue plaque on the wall outside lists a number of the library's eminent members.

MANCHESTER ART GALLERY   A little further down Mosley Street is the Manchester Art Gallery which was originally built for the Manchester Institute for Science, Literature and the Arts, by Charles Barry 1824-35. The Ionic columns of the main entrance replicate those on Thomas Harrison's Portico Library nearby. Much of the wealth that the city derived from the cotton industry was invested in art collections of the era, many of which remain in the gallery today.

In 1882 the then owners offered the building, with contents, to Manchester Corporation for free with the stipulation that the council agreed to spend £2000 a year for twenty years on new works of art. By the end of the nineteenth century an impressive collection had been assembled.

44

Today the museum is one of the finest art museums in the country with its collections of fine art that span six centuries and include amongst its modern and contemporary pieces an outstanding collection of Pre-Raphaelite works. Exhibits include paintings in oils and watercolours, sculptures, miniatures, prints, ceramics, glass, enamels, furniture, metalwork, wallpapers, arms and armour. The exhibitions are regularly renewed and updated to showcase the artistry, tastes and techniques across the generations.

PICCADILLY STATION ('the Gateway to Manchester')

Piccadilly Station is Manchester's major rail terminus. The first station at this location, Store Street, was completed in 1842. From here trains began to run to London which revolutionised travel for northerners as the time for the journey was cut from a twenty-four-hour stagecoach trip, which included an overnight stop, to a nine-and-a-half hour train journey. It was renamed London Road in 1860, enlarged in 1866 and further extended in the 1880s when the current roof was added. By then travel time to London was down to four and a quarter hours.

Below: The 'lazy S' shaped building alongside the ramped station approach is Gateway House, an office block built as part of station refurbishment work 1967-69, after which it was renamed Manchester Piccadilly.

As part of the development of the city's Metrolink system an interchange was constructed in the station's undercroft. When the system first opened in 1992 it ran from Piccadilly to Victoria Station and on to Bury, with the route to Altrincham branching off at Piccadilly Gardens.

The refurbishment of the station in the mid sixties accompanied the electrification of the line to London, cutting journey times between the now named Piccadilly Station and London Euston to two hours thirty-five minutes. Since then, further modifications to the line and timetable have seen travel times on some trains reduced to just over two hours.

THE OLD FIRE AND POLICE STATION – LONDON ROAD

This magnificent triangular building, built around a courtyard, was constructed 1901-6 by Woodhouse, Willoughby and Langham, a team seemingly formed to develop this building only and disbanded on its completion. This huge terracotta-faced, Accrington brick structure was innovative in its planning. In addition to the required operations facilities it contained working and living quarters for forty firemen, policemen and their families with its own library, gymnasium, bank and stables. It was vacated by the Fire Service in 1986 and has been more or less empty ever since. However in 2015 it was purchased by developers with firm plans for restoration. Hopefully it will not be long before this iconic Edwardian marvel is brought back to life.

THE ETIHAD STADIUM

Built to host the 2002 Commonwealth Games the stadium was subsequently converted to host football and leased to Manchester City Football Club who moved to the ground for the start of the 2003-4 season. Extensions and alterations have seen the capacity of the ground increased from the Commonwealth Games' 38,000 to 60,000 with plans to add more seats in progress. This has made the stadium an attractive venue for the world's leading music acts such as Coldplay and Bruce Springsteen who both played here in 2012 and returned in 2016.

PICCADILLY GARDENS

Once an area that boasted wonderfully colourful gardens, the redevelopments that have taken place over the years have met with much warranted criticism. However, for many this piece of open space, which is the largest in the city centre, is the very heart of the city. This grassy area is surrounded by cafés, bars and restaurants and plays host to many of the city's events and concerts throughout the year. With a Manchester Metrolink station and bus station alongside it is also plays an important role in the city's transport system.

Right: Prominent in the 'Gardens' is a large bronze statue of Queen Victoria that was created by sculptor Edward Onslow Ford as a tribute to the queen. It was unveiled in 1901, ten months after her death.

On the reverse of the monument, overlooking the 'gardens' and sheltered from the pigeons, is an evocative statue of 'Motherhood'. This beautiful bronze depicts a young woman holding two sleeping infants to her chest. The plinth below contains this most appropriate quote from Shakespeare's *Henry IV* Part II 'Let me bear your love, I'll bear your cares'.

Edward Onslow Ford specialised in carving white marble but bronze was chosen for the then industrial Manchester, due to the bad air pollution caused by the smoking chimneys of the many surrounding factories.

Manchester Markets are often held in the 'Gardens' with food from all round the world available to passers-by.

City Tower (formerly the Sunley Building) is a product of the 1960s desire to construct tower blocks. This 30 storey skyscraper, which rises above Piccadilly Plaza aside Piccadilly Gardens, was designed for Bernard Sunley & Sons by Covell, Matthews & Partners. The proliferation of antennae and satellite dishes on and around the building make it Manchester's main broadcast transmission site. The tower has recently been fully refurbished with work including the replacement of all window panels and protective white paint applied to the side façades. Though not the tallest building in Manchester it does provide the highest commercial office space in the city.

THE SHAKESPEARE PUB

Hidden just off the beaten paths around Piccadilly Gardens, on Fountain Street, is this curious public house. Looking every bit an historic structure this mock timber-framed pub was actually built in 1923 by W. Johnson & Sons incorporating parts of a demolished building in Chester. It is thought that the carvings and ornamentations are authentic seventeenth century works.

THE ASHTON CANAL

Envious of the Duke of Bridgewater's success in transporting his coal into Manchester via his own canal, the mine owners around Ashton sought to emulate his achievements. The Ashton Canal opened in 1796 and from a large basin in Piccadilly, formed a link between Manchester's canals and the Huddersfield Narrow and Peak Forest Canals. As with canals generally the decline in goods traffic saw its eventual closure in 1961, but it was saved from dereliction in the 1970s when volunteers cleared the canal of the weeds and rubbish that had accumulated. In 1974 they reopened the waterway into the heart of the city where now the Piccadilly Village residential development has been built on the canal side.

ALLIOTT VERDON ROE
(1877-1958)
and
HUMPHREY VERDON ROE
(1879-1949)
formed the A.V. Roe & Co (Avro)
aircraft company on 1st January
1910 and opened their first
workshop here.
117

ANCOATS

This area is oft regarded as the world's first industrial suburb with its mills, housing (including workhouses), churches, pubs and community facilities all built on a Georgian street grid, all born out of the needs of the economic and industrial expansion of Manchester in the late eighteenth century. The rapidly increasing population demanded more housing and the developing textile industry was seeking sites where the new steam-driven textile machinery could be fully utilised. Mills were built along the proposed route of the Rochdale Canal in anticipation of the mutual benefits that would result.

Brownsfield Mill, which dates from 1825, was constructed as a room and power mill for multiple occupancy. As the blue plaque that graces the building records, this was the site of the first workshop of the Avro aircraft manufacturer. Founded in 1910 the company went on to produce aircraft at sites in Woodford, Chadderton, Trafford Park and Alexandria Park. The Manchester, Lincoln, Shackleton and Vulcan were some of the twentieth-century's most famous British aircraft, all products of A.V. Roe and Company (Avro).

Royal Mill. This was one of the last cotton-spinning mills constructed in this part of Manchester. Built in 1912, on part of a site previously occupied by earlier mills, it was originally known as New Old Mill. Following a visit by King George VI and Queen Elizabeth in 1942 it was renamed Royal Mill. After decades of neglect a restoration project that commenced in 2003 has seen this and other surrounding mills converted to flats, offices and shops with a number of original features retained and a spectacular glass atrium constructed in their midst.

ANCOATS –
GEORGE LEIGH STREET

Much of the housing in Ancoats was built on land owned by the Leigh family giving this street its name. The earliest properties were built back-to-back with two-up two-down terraces following later.

The houses on George Leigh Street and the adjacent Anita Street, were built in the late 1890s by the Manchester City Council, some of the first with their internal layouts dictated by the act that required councils to provide accommodation with separate bedrooms for girls, boys and parents.

The tall building in the background is Victoria Square, the first example of municipal housing in Manchester, which opened in 1894 providing accommodation for over 800 people in 237 double and 48 single tenements. The building now offers retirement/sheltered housing.

Art has not been forgotten in the regeneration of the area with this sculpture of a retired couple sitting outside No. 51 George Leigh Street. Former millworkers sit in the sun reading the following –

'The dawn of the morn for glory
The hush of the night for peace
In the garden at eve' says the story
God walks and his smile brings release.'

CUTTING ROOM SQUARE

In the heart of the regenerated Ancoats is Cutting Room Square, dominated by St Peter's church and watched over by five giant monoliths.

The church was built in 1859, a time when Ancoats was a bustling, overcrowded industrial workshop. It was the first Anglican church in what was a predominantly Roman Catholic area. With attendances on the wane closure came in 1960. It has now been fully restored and whilst it is a permanent rehearsal and recording venue for the Hallé Orchestra it also serves as a resource for the whole community.

Each of the five monoliths, in the square, have an enlarged photograph, taken by Ancoats artist-in-residence Dan Dubowitz, depicting scenes from the cutting rooms within the textile mills just before they were demolished.

HALLÉ ST PETER'S

The versatility of this eye-catching venue is clearly demonstrated in these next photographs. Those below show the hall floor is clear as preparations for a tea-dance are in progress. A few days later (over the page) the Hallé Orchestra has returned for a full rehearsal.

The most recent installation is the 'Eye of Helios' stained glass Rose window, by the renowned British glass artist Derek Hunt. The central motif is of the sun radiating outwards with vibrant shades of blue and green.

METHODIST WOMEN'S NIGHT SHELTER

On the corner of George Leigh Street and Great Ancoats Street is a slender building, designed by William Sharp. This was the Ancoats Methodist Women's Night Shelter that opened in 1899. The ground floor, of this four-storey building, served as a coffee tavern with the upper floors given over to providing night shelter defined as a home for women needing 'further care and discipline'. It also offered accommodation to domestic servants seeking an alternative 'roof over their head' to that provided by lodging houses where protection was minimal.

In 1960 the building was taken over by the Daily Express for offices, next to their existing building.

The impressive building next door is the Hudson Building, built as a warehouse in 1924, but now converted to flats.

THE DAILY EXPRESS BUILDING

For many the Daily Express building is the most striking futurist art deco building in the city. Designed for Lord Beaverbrook by Sir Owen Williams it was built in 1939 and was one of the first to embrace the then new design concept of curtain walling. With its all glass front, a mixture of translucent glass and black glass and rounded corners, the printing presses at work made an impressive sight to passers-by, particularly after dark. This was home to the newspaper for over sixty years during which time the building was extended a number of times. The presses stopped rolling in the late 1980s when the newspaper left Manchester and the building lay derelict until conversion work, to offices, commenced in the mid '90s.

THE NORTHERN QUARTER

This is the creative area of the city with impressive artwork round every corner, much of which changes regularly.

Above left: A challenger for the largest piece of art work is this larger than life representation of a blue tit that graces a wall off Newton Street. It is the work of graphic artist and designer Faunagraphic and was commissioned in 2011 by Converse as part of their worldwide Wall-to-Wall project.

Above right: One of the most impressive examples of urban artwork is this substantial mural that adorns the gable of the Ridelow bike shop on Church Street. It was painted in 2011 by Subism Collective, a multifaceted independent creative business that works with artists around the world. This was a five-day project for four of their artists who created this Earth, Wind, Fire and Water themed illustration.

Among other art forms displayed across the 'quarter' are these tile mosaics in the window recesses of Afflecks Palace. These are the work of Mark Kennedy, a local artist renowned for his mosaic portraits of people and products affiliated with the city. Even *Coronation Street*'s Hilda Ogden has her famous 'flying ducks' immortalised.

AFFLECKS

An indoor market that is for those looking for something a bit different. It was opened in 1982 by local hairdresser James Walsh who had an interest in fashion. It occupies the premises of the former Affleck & Brown Department Store, hence the name. They had started out as a drapery business back in the 1860s. Though ownership changed hands in 2008 this labyrinthine Victorian building has remained an Aladdin's cave of goodies.

Wandering this rabbit warren full of independent shops and stalls you are able to purchase fetish fashions, new designer clothing, surf wear, accessories, jewellery general memorabilia, musical instruments and much more. You can also have henna tattoos applied and/or piercings of every variety. You can then rest your weary limbs in one of the cafés.

SMITHFIELD WHOLESALE FISH MARKET These historic façades that surround this new residential development are virtually all that remains of the Smithfield Wholesale Fish Market that opened in 1873. It was designed by Speakman, Son and Hickson and included ornate ironwork gates by Hodkinson, Poynton & Lester and sculpted friezes by Joseph Bonehill. It closed in the 1970s when the roof and some of the internal walls were removed. Some of the wrought iron columns remain. The original role of the building being exactly what you see on the walls as the friezes show scenes of fishing at sea, landing the catch and selling it on.

MANCHESTER CRAFT AND DESIGN CENTRE Built at the same time as the nearby Wholesale Fish Market was a Retail Fish Market but this building has survived intact and now houses the Manchester Craft and Design Centre. The fish trade ceased in 1973 and Manchester City Council converted the derelict building into the Manchester Craft Village in 1982, retaining two of the original fishmongers' booths on the ground floor. Located just a few minutes from the city centre this self-claimed 'oasis of calm' features two floors of contemporary craft studios in and amongst some original and quirky fixtures and fittings.

THE CIS TOWER AND 1 ANGEL SQUARE

The Co-operative that started out in a small shop in Lancashire is now a worldwide movement. Having been in Manchester since the 1800s, between 1959-62 it constructed what is arguably Manchester's finest office block of the time. The 25-storey CIS Tower (Cooperative Insurance) was designed by G.S. Hay of the CWS and Gordon Tait of Sir John Burnet, Tait & Partners. When built the windowless service tower was constructed as a steel frame clad in reinforced concrete and mosaic. Glass, aluminium and black enamelled steel were chosen for the 'office' block, much more suitable for keeping clean in the Manchester atmosphere. The mosaic cladding proved to be a maintenance nightmare from soon after construction and was eventually replaced with a weatherproof cladding incorporating photovoltaic panels.

The 'green' policy has continued with the Cooperative Group's stunning new headquarters, 1 Angel Square. Designed by 3D Reid and opened in 2012 it is not only eye catching but one of the most environmentally friendly buildings in the world.

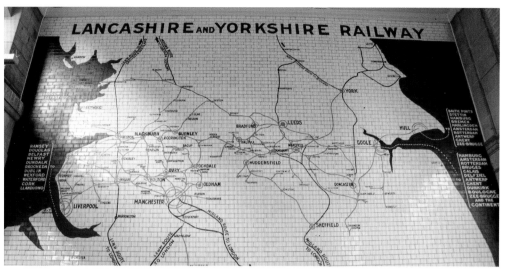

VICTORIA STATION Opened in 1844 as Hunts Bank, the terminus of the Manchester & Leeds Railway was soon connected to the Liverpool & Manchester line and serving all destinations to the north west and east of the country. A small part of the original single-storey station, which was designed by Robert Stephenson, still survives. The station was enlarged, for the Lancashire & Yorkshire Railway, in 1909, and the main building from these works still remains. Interesting retained features are the glazed canopy along the street frontage and the glazed brick panel, beside the northern entrance, which has painted on it a map of the L&YR railway network.

Once the most attractive of Manchester's stations, Victoria has undergone many changes in more recent years. In the 1980s plans were unveiled to link the station with Piccadilly as part of the new Metrolink system. With BR subsequently rerouting services to Piccadilly, many of Victoria's platforms became redundant and eventually made way for a new concert arena. The development of the currently named Manchester Arena coupled with the introduction of the Metrolink lines did little for the overall appearance of the station.

2013 saw the start of a two year modernisation programme that was completed in August 2015. The works included electrification of the through routes, a new Metrolink stop with additional platform, the replacement of the original train shed roof with a new 'all-over' roof and the restoration of Listed features. Network Rail proclaims that they have 'transformed Manchester Victoria into a modern and exciting gateway to the city'. Thankfully the Edwardian booking hall survives as does the range that consists of a restaurant, domed refreshment room and bookstall, including the gold mosaic lettering on a turquoise background that identifies their location.

MANCHESTER METROLINK

This was the first modern street running rail system in the United Kingdom. Opened in phases from 1992 the network now comprises seven lines linking the city centre with termini at Altrincham, Bury, East Didsbury, Eccles, Manchester Airport and Rochdale. The first phase included the street section that linked the then separate 'cross-country' rail networks that radiated from Victoria Station, north of the city centre, with the 'intercity' services that operated out of Piccadilly Station to the south. The line leaves Victoria Station and passes through Shudehill where, in 2006, a new interchange was created with a bus station and car park built alongside.

The tram lines then head towards Market Street (left) before entering Piccadilly Gardens (top). At Piccadilly the lines to the station and Ashton-under-Lyne split from those that continue through to Deansgate Castlefield (above) after which the lines to East Didsbury, Altrincham and Eccles (including Media City) branch off.

Work has now commenced on a second cross city link between Victoria Station and St Peter's Square via Corporation Street, Cross Street and Princess Street. The first phase which included a station at Exchange Square was completed and opened at the end of 2015. This new connection takes the trams through the area devastated by an IRA bomb in 1996 and past the now famous postbox that remained standing amongst the carnage. The plaque affixed to the box reads 'This postbox remained standing almost undamaged on June 15th 1996 when this area was devastated by a bomb. This box was removed during the rebuilding of the city centre and was returned to its original site on November 22nd 1999.'

The entrance from Exchange Square.

THE ARNDALE

The Uk's largest inner-city shopping centre is also perhaps the most unloved with its bland buff tile clad façades earning it, when first built, the nickname the 'biggest toilet in Britain'! Subsequent remodelling work, including repairs after the 1996 bomb, have 'softened' some of the elevations. Designed by Wilson & Womersley and built in phases between 1972-80, this large site comprises around 240 shops and major department stores, restaurants, fast food outlets and a 1450 space car park.

This panoramic view was taken from the Shudehill multi-storey car park.

MANCHESTER TOWN HALL AND ALBERT SQUARE The grandest and most imposing building in the region. Designed by Alfred Waterhouse (see also the Refuge Assurance/Palace Hotel building) construction of the Town Hall commenced in 1868 and took nine years to complete. The 'Gothic' style structure was built in brick faced externally with stone from West Yorkshire quarries and the façade also includes statues honouring figures from Manchester's past including General Agricola, the Roman who founded Manchester in AD 79.

The giant clock tower above the main entrance is 286 feet high and the minute hand is 10 feet long! The spiked golden ball atop the spire symbolises an 'about to burst' cotton bud and the sun, for it was said that whenever the sun shone Manchester had business.

You have only to glimpse the main entrance vestibule to establish the magnificence and beauty of Waterhouse's internal architecture and decoration for this building. Statues of John Dalton (below right) and James Prescott Joule (below left) keep an eye on all visitors.

Albert Square was laid out between 1868 and 1877 around the imposing Town Hall, becoming the setting for many demonstrations and civic events. There are a number of statues in the square but the focal point has to be the Albert Memorial. This sandstone shrine, designed by Thomas Worthington to house the Mathew Noble statue of the Prince Consort, was officially unveiled in January 1867.

The Square also boasts a fountain that was commissioned for the Diamond Jubilee of Queen Victoria. This was also designed by Thomas Worthington and was completed in time for the celebrations in 1897. After thirty years it was moved to Heaton Park where it remained for seventy years falling into disrepair. After restoration it was returned to the Square in 1997.

Opposite: An extension to the Town Hall, designed by Emmanuel Vincent Harris, was added in 1938 and is linked via a number of elegant bridges.

This impressive block of buildings along the southern side of the Square includes St Andrew's Chambers, built in 1872 by George Redmayne, for the Scottish Widows Assurance Society on the left. Next to that is Carlton House which also dates from 1872. This was originally called Bridgewater Buildings when it housed the headquarters of the Bridgewater Canal Company. It was also home of the architectural practise of Clegg and Knowles who designed the adjacent Albert Chambers in 1873 for the Manchester Corporation Gasworks. On the right is the decidedly Venetian Gothic-styled Memorial Hall which was of course another design by Thomas Worthington. This was erected 1863-6 and had been commissioned to commemorate the Great Ejection of 1662 when 2000 ministers were expelled from the Church of England for refusing to submit to the Oath of Conformity. As well as providing for religious instruction it became a home for free thinkers and the younger members of the Unitarian Church. Having been derelict for most of the last decade it has now been restored as a popular restaurant.

Along Princess Street on the north side of the Square is this Flemish-style building with Dutch gables, which was designed by architects Waddington and Dunkerley and built for the Northern Assurance Company in 1902.

MANCHESTER CENTRAL LIBRARY

The city's main municipal library is a grand building in a great location. Designed by Emmanuel Vincent Harris as part of the civic rebuilding scheme of the 1930s, associated with the Town Hall extension, it is a classically proportioned building but not particularly practical for its intended use.

It was closed in 2010 for major refurbishment which was to considerably increase the areas of the building accessible to the public including the addition of a modern staircase and lift. What has been created is a '21st century book lover's paradise for the digital age'.

The most impressive room which has remained intact and acoustically improved is the first floor reading room. This beautifully designed room encircled by twenty eight Tuscan columns with an Italianate well head as a central feature has also retained the original desks complete with their eighty-year-old graffiti. The words around the dome are from the Old Testament's Book of Proverbs.

The second floor is occupied by the Arts and Music Libraries.

The Library reopened on completion of the Ryder Architects-designed refurbishment works, in 2014.

ST MARY'S CHURCH, MANCHESTER'S HIDDEN GEM

The church built on this site in 1794 was the first purpose-built Catholic church in England since the Reformation. It was purposely sited amidst what was then an area of intensive poor housing. The church that stands today was built in 1848 by Weightman and Hadfield after the previous building had virtually collapsed. The magnificent interior sculptures date from the 1860s and were carried out by a Mr Lane of Preston. The elaborate marble carvings earning the church the name 'Hidden Gem' which has been used ever since.

Around the perimeter are a unique series of modern art paintings by the late Royal Academy member Norman Adams, seen by many as the leading British religious painter of the twentieth century. The 14 pictures are imaginative depictions of the Passion of Christ.

The church was completely refurbished in the early 1990s.

EXCHANGE SQUARE

Created in the aftermath of the 1996 bomb this triangular 'Square' is in the heart of the 'new' shopping and leisure area. Around its perimeter are the historic Printworks, Corn Exchange and Shambles opposite the Arndale Centre and the first Selfridges store to be opened outside of London. It is now also on the route of the new cross city Metrolink line.

THE PRINTWORKS

This was the largest newspaper office in the world for much of the twentieth century. It was home to *Manchester Evening Chronicle* and *Sunday Graphic* in addition to housing the northern offices of the *Daily Telegraph* and *Sunday Times*. The first newspapers were printed here in 1873. It was named Kemsley House when taken over by Kemsley Papers in 1937 becoming Thomson House twenty-two years later.

1985 saw the building change hands once more but for just one pound. The new owner was the now disgraced Robert Maxwell who, as predicted at the time, closed it down the following year. It was derelict for the next ten years but was purchased, after the bomb, by a Birmingham development company. They redeveloped the project within the existing façades to create a leisure complex with a multi-screen cinema, bars and famous restaurants.

THE CORN EXCHANGE

Whilst a Corn Exchange has stood on this site since 1837, the current substantial building dates from 1903 and was designed by Ball & Elce. It ceased trading in the 1960s and soon became home to a very popular flea market with new-age mystics, books, record stalls and second hand clothing markets. The upper floor's small offices were occupied by small businesses including aprivate detective.

Having suffered considerable bomb damage in 1996 it was rebuilt as a shopping mall and seemed to lose much of its character in the process.

Over the last couple of years a 30 million pound redevelopment programme has transformed the building into a café and restaurant hub with a grand hotel due to open shortly.

The 'new' Shambles Square was created in 1999 around the relocated Old Wellington Inn and Sinclair's Oyster Bar. The Old Wellington Inn building is thought to date back to 1552 when it was built in a street of medieval buildings collectively known as the Shambles. In its early life it was a draper's shop with living quarters, becoming a pub, called the Vintner's Arms in 1830. It acquired the Old Wellington Inn title in 1865.

The building, known as Sinclair's Oyster Bar since 1845, is much younger dating from 1720. Having remarkably survived the Second World War, both buildings were 'jacked-up' approximately 5 feet on a steel and concrete foundation, as part of the redevelopment of the old market area in the 1970s.

In the wake of the IRA bomb, which they survived, it was decided to move them 'brick by brick' to make way for the redevelopment of the Marks and Spencer site. Their new home is on the edge of Exchange Square near to the Cathedral.

URBIS – THE NATIONAL FOOTBALL MUSEUM

This unique glass structure was designed by Ian Simpson and built in 2000-1 as part of the area's regeneration.

Commissioned as a 'Museum of the City' but failing to attract sufficient visitors to a variety of exhibits and special events, it closed in 2010. Following a complete re-fit it re-opened in 2012 as a permanent home for a National Football Museum which contains the largest collection of football memorabilia with over 140,000 objects spread over its three floors.

It is worth a visit to travel the indoor funicular, a glass lift that climbs at an angle to serve each level.

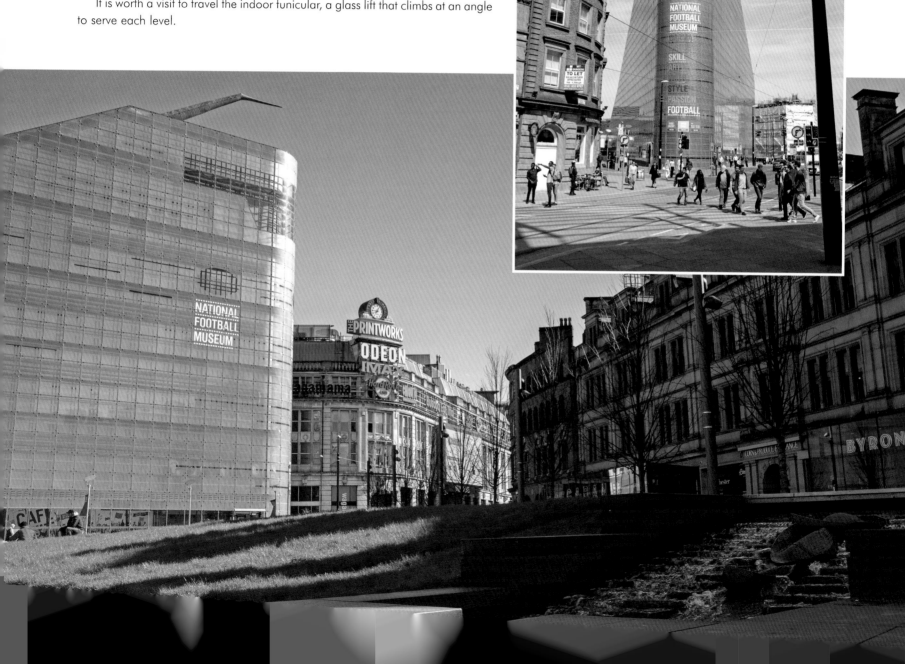

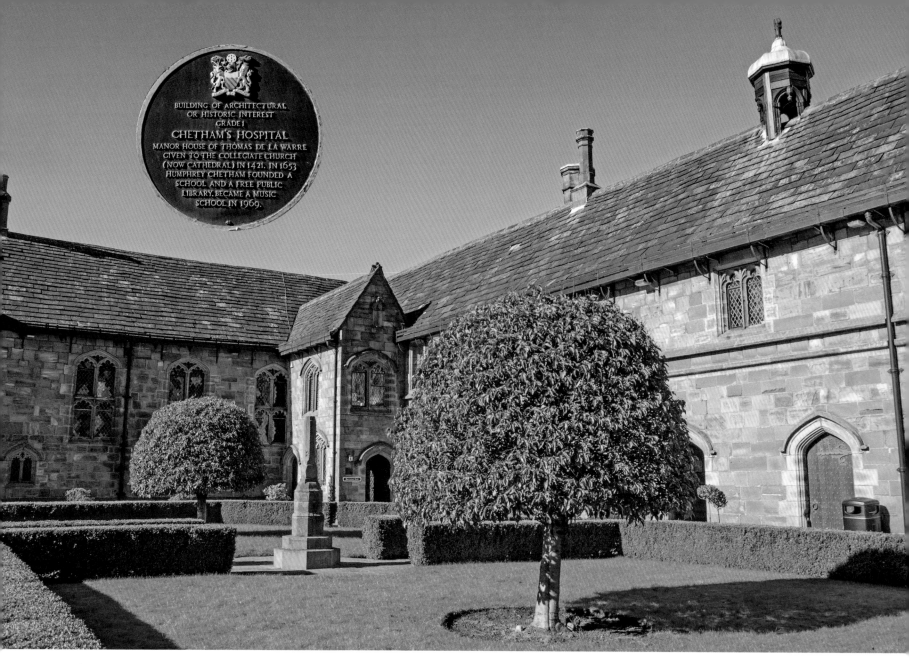

CHETHAM'S LIBRARY

The oldest surviving public library in Britain, founded in 1653, was established by the will of Humphrey Chetham a prosperous Manchester textile merchant, banker and landowner. He also made provision for the setting up of a school for forty poor boys which is now a specialist music school known all over the world.

The building that houses the library is much older having been built in 1421 to house the priests of the Manchester Collegiate Church and is one of the most complete medieval complexes in the north-west of England.

What was soon assembled was a major collection of books and manuscripts covering the whole range of available knowledge, rivalling those in the libraries of Oxford and Cambridge. The library was housed on the first floor to avoid the risk of damp and newly acquired books were chained to the book cases, or presses for security. In the mid eighteenth century chaining was abandoned and gates were fitted to prevent theft.

Chetham's also provided funds for the setting up of five small libraries, designed to be chained and housed in wooden chests, and placed in the parish churches of Manchester. Only two of these libraries survive and that from Gorton was returned in 1984. It is on display in the Reading Room which also has, above the fireplace, an elaborate heraldic and emblematic display commemorating Chetham and his foundation.

MANCHESTER CATHEDRAL

The origins of the church on this site were in a charter that the then Lord of the Manor of Manchester, Thomas de la Warre, obtained in 1421 to establish a church with an attached college of priests (Chetham's). Built between 1422 and 1458, the new church was dedicated to St Mary, St George and St Denys. After becoming a cathedral in 1847 there was much improvement work carried out during the rest of the 1800s. During the Second World War a German bomb destroyed most of the north east of the Cathedral with substantial damage to the rest of the structure. Restoration took almost twenty years to complete.

More recently a new underfloor heating system has been installed and the work has included the replacement of much of the floor. A pop-up cathedral was erected alongside to enable Sunday services to continue during the works.

The Cathedral has throughout its history been central to Manchester life. In the early years the nave of the building would have been largest covered space in Manchester and would have hosted many of the its public functions. This tradition continues today: in addition to its day-to-day religious commitments the building has recently seen concerts by artists that include Alicia Keys and Elbow, performed within its walls.

NEW CATHEDRAL STREET

Opened in 2003, the pedestrianised New Cathedral Street completed the transformation of the area of the city devastated by the 1996 bomb. With Selfridges and Marks and Spencer along one side and stylish stores such as Harvey Nichols, Zara and Burberry opposite, it claims to provide the ultimate shopping experience.

Shoppers are often entertained by one of Manchester's most popular musical street entertainers, THE HOOCHIE COOCHIE MANcunian!

Music of all persuasions can be heard all around the city on most shopping days throughout the year.

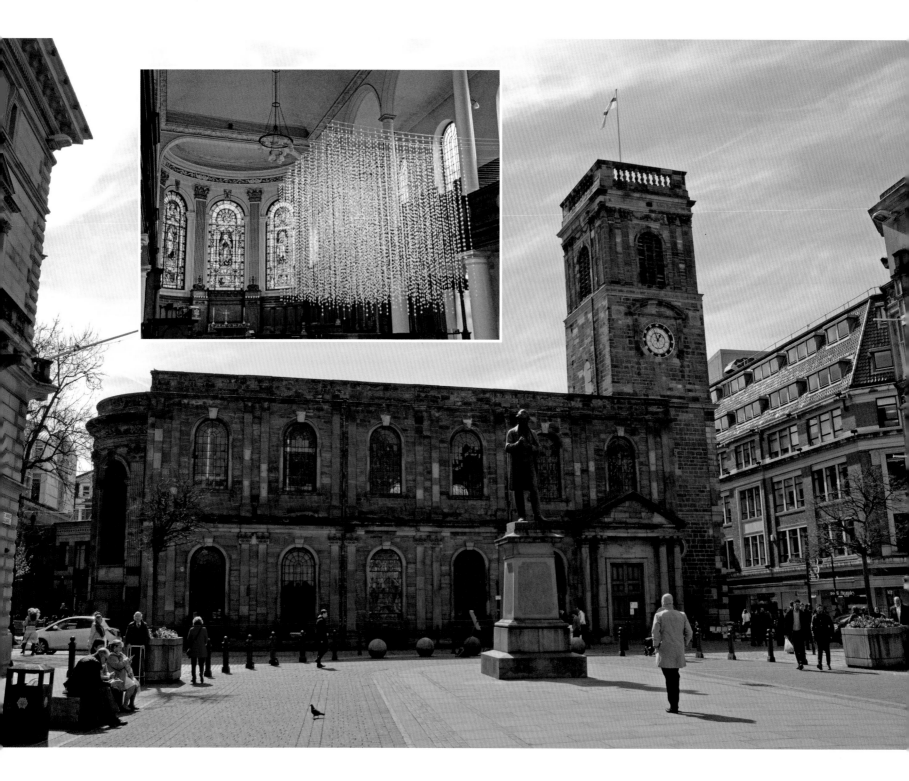

ST ANN'S CHURCH, ST ANN'S SQUARE

The church and the Square on which it stands were the first major developments away from the medieval settlements around the Cathedral. Consecrated in 1712 St Ann's dedication not only refers to the saint but also acknowledges Lady Ann Bland, the church's patron, who had provided the money for its construction. Externally the building was the first church in Manchester to use the Classical style of architecture and the tower is regarded as the traditional centre of the city. The elegant interior has galleries set on Tuscan columns and fascinating examples of stained glass. The three east windows are of particular interest, dating from 1887-89 and being by a Manchester-based artist, Frederick Shields. The centre one depicts Jesus Christ as the good shepherd, with Moses and St Paul on either side.

THE ROYAL EXCHANGE

This monumental structure, that stands between St Ann's Square and Cross Street, highlights the significance of cotton in the creation of Manchester. From the erection of the first building in 1729 through a number of rebuilds and extensions, the last of which was during the First World War, the Exchange developed to become the industry's head office with a trading floor that, by the 1920s, was controlling 80% of the world's finished cotton trade. Around the hall there were floors with around 250 offices, over 30 shops, restaurants and a post office.

Trading continued until the 1960s when the Lancashire cotton Industry finally succumbed to overseas competition and the Royal Exchange closed its doors on 31 December 1968.

Whilst the shops and offices continued to provide rent the vast hall was empty and attracted fears that the building could be demolished.

However the 1969 Theatre Company moved in and they commissioned the architects, Levitt, Bernstein Associates to build a theatre. Their ingenious design was for a seven-sided steel and glass module suspended from four columns with seating for 740. This made it the largest theatre-in-the-round in the world and on the 15 September 1976 Sir Laurence Olivier was able to 'declare this theatre open'. Save for the period of repairs following the 1996 bomb when the company played at a Castlefield, the theatre has been a tremendous success opening its doors to theatre productions from all over this country and beyond.

MR. THOMAS'S CHOP HOUSE

Another building with elevations on both Cross Street and St Ann's Square is this one. Chop houses were establishments where businessmen dined and conducted their affairs over hearty, home cooked meals, washed down with fine wine. The original building on the site was a slender Georgian town house. Mr Thomas Studd (hence the name) first opened it as a public house and restaurant in 1870. Having commissioned architect Robert Walker to rebuild and extend the original premises this version of Mr. Thomas's opened in 1901.

This was one of the first cast-iron-framed buildings in the city and is clad in a mix of decorative terracotta blocks and Accrington brick.

Internally the finishes are almost completely original. The arches and Victorian tiling being the Mr. Thomas's building's most distinguishing features.

The Chop House's 'Welcome' information sheet refers to the *New York Times* view of the establishment as 'probably Manchester's most venerable pub'. It goes on to confirm the current management's intention for it to be Manchester's '"most welcoming pub'. My own experience when seeking permission to take these photographs leads me to applaud their success in achieving their aim.

DEANSGATE, BARTON ARCADE

Hidden behind the façade of Barton's Building on Deansgate is the Victorian Barton Arcade which houses exclusive shops and offices. Built in 1871, by Corbett, Raby & Sawyer, there are three tiers of balconies with ornamental balustrades and mahogany handrails that curve around what is a 'U' shaped glass and iron shopping arcade. The decorative ironwork was the work of the Macfarlane's foundry in Glasgow. Extensive restoration work was carried out in the 1980s and whilst the original shop fronts and decorative tiled floor were lost, the building itself is still thought to be the best example of this type of structure in the country.

HOUSE OF FRASER (KENDALS)

This striking art deco building was built by J. S. Beaumont and dates from 1939. Kendals have traded on Deansgate since the 1830s. At that time they occupied the building opposite the present one (now a branch of Waterstones). They expanded into premises on this site across the road in the late nineteenth century. The two sites were linked via an underground passage.

House of Fraser took control of Kendal Milne in 1959 but the name was not changed until after completion of the major refurbishment works in 2005.

The store, which epitomised style long before the likes of Harvey Nichols and Selfridges appeared on the high street is still stubbornly referred to as Kendals by Mancunians. This local affection for the name dates back to the time of previous owners, Harrods. They had tried to change the name but failed in the face of opposition from staff and customers.

PARSONAGE GARDENS

Just behind Kendals is a little oasis of trees, grass, flower beds and pathways. A sun trap to temporarily relieve the stress and strain of office work or to give the throbbing feet of shoppers a well deserved rest.

The garden's name reflects the area's association with the church of St Mary (Manchester Cathedral).

KING STREET

Once the city's financial district and the heart of the North West banking industry, King Street has latterly become progressively dominated by expensive shops, a leading destination for shoppers seeking designer goods and luxury brands. Named in 1735 in support of the exiled Stuart kings, King Street was initially a largely residential street but by the 1830s the properties had begun to be taken over by the business community. Many buildings were rebuilt during the reign of Queen Victoria but one eighteenth-century building that has survived is now the last Georgian mansion in Central Manchester (photo bottom right). It dates from 1736 when built as a residence, becoming a bank in 1788. The 'Old Exchange Building' (inset) which includes a covered passageway from St Ann's Place (below), was designed by Royle & Bennetts in 1897. Its name derives from its predecessor on the site that had provided accommodation for the Cotton Exchange around 1800.

In 1976 the section west of Cross Street was the first city centre street to become pedestrians only, with St Ann's Square following suit in the early 1980s.

Unfortunately the retail developments at New Cathedral Street and Spinningfields have adversely affected trade here and what was once known as the Bond Street of the North has unfortunately seen many shops closed in recent years.

Above: East of Cross Street was the location for the majority of the Manchester branches of the major banks leaving a legacy of handsome office blocks lining the street. The building on the right was the first permanent provincial branch of the Bank of England designed by Charles Cockerell in 1846. In the distance, across the top of King Street, on Spring Gardens, is the Lancashire and Yorkshire Bank building that dates from 1888.

The large Portland stone structure in the centre of the photograph is the steel-framed Ship Canal House built by Harry S. Fairhurst and opened in 1924. The 36-mile long Manchester Ship Canal had opened to shipping in 1894.

Some of the buildings continue to deal with commercial finances but others have been transformed into exclusive designer outlets and splendid bars and restaurants.

Left: On the corner of King Street and Spring Gardens is the former 'Reform Club' by Edward Salomons (1870-1). This Venetian-style sandstone building is one of the largest surviving provincial clubhouses in the country. It opened in 1871 when William Gladstone was guest of honour and at its peak included Winston Churchill and Lloyd George among its membership. Indeed Churchill gave his 1906 election victory speech from the balcony, having won the Manchester North West seat. It closed in 1988 and is now home to expensive shops, restaurants and a night club.

At the junction of Spring Gardens and York Street, across from the former Reform Club, is 'Browns Bar and Brasserie', housed in what was once the imposing banking hall of Parr's Bank, built by Charles Heathcote in 1902. This baroque red sandstone building has been described as one of 'extraordinary flamboyance' and whilst enjoying afternoon tea it is easy to see why. Internally the art nouveau detailing, particularly the wrought ironwork, is beautiful. At the entrance is a foyer in mahogany with Ionic columns framing the doors that open into the opulent banking hall itself with its green marble walls and richly moulded plasterwork to the ceilings. Some original stained glass also survives. Browns opened here in 2011; prior to that the venue was one of Manchester's most famous pubs, the 'Athenaeum'.

THE JOHN RYLANDS LIBRARY

Manchester's first multi-millionaire, John Rylands was an extremely successful cotton manufacturer and merchant whose philanthropy was well known at home and abroad. Following his death in 1888 his wife, Enriqueta Rylands, wanted to create a suitable memorial to her late husband and commissioned architect Basil Champneys. Together they designed and built a library to house Rylands's small collection of theological books. Opened in 1900, what they created is today acclaimed to be one of the best examples of neo-Gothic architecture in Europe and arguably one of the finest libraries in the world. Since 1972 the library has been a part of Manchester University and was extensively restored between 2004-7.

The main structure is built from Cumbrian sandstone, which varies in colour between rose pink and grey. Timberwork is in the best Polish oak sought from the Gdansk region. The whole interior is enhanced with white moulded plasterwork and ornate cast brass, art nouveau-style light fittings and other metalwork. The library was one of the city's first to be lit by electricity which was originally generated on site, connection to the 'mains' coming in the 1950s.

The historic Reading Room is spectacular with a magnificent vaulted ceiling more than 40 feet above its aisle which, at either end, is watched over by Cassidy's marble statues of John and Enriqueta Rylands. On each side are alcoves for personal study and the whole floor is 30 feet above street level to acoustically insulate it from the passing traffic outside which when constructed would have been the sound of horses hooves on cobblestones.

The collections of books and manuscripts within, dating back to the third millennium BC, cover a vast range of subjects and encompass all landmarks of printing techniques on most kind of materials ever used. These include clay, papyrus, linen, parchment, paper, wood, vellum, bone, bark, bamboo, palm leaf, copper and ivory.

Since becoming part of the University of Manchester this memorial to the memory of John Rylands is now the third largest academic library in the United Kingdom and home to more than 250,000 printed volumes and over a million manuscripts and archival items.

THE SAWYER'S ARMS

On the corner with Bridge Street is the Sawyers Arms public house, with its striking Victorian exterior consisting of maroon and cream tiling. Having gained its first licence in 1730 it is reputed to be one of Manchester's oldest pubs and is unique in retaining its original name since records began in 1734.

PETER STREET

Three buildings of historic significance. Furthest away is the Free Trade Hall that was built between 1853 and 1856 by Edward Walters as a hall suitable for 'literary, religious, musical and other purposes'. Now forming part of a large hotel the 'halls' have, over the years, been the setting for everything from political rallies to rock concerts and was home to the Hallé Orchestra for many years.

Next comes the 'Theatre Royal' which is the city's oldest surviving theatre dating from 1845 although in recent years it has been in use as a night club.

Nearest the camera, and much younger, dating from 1911, is St George's House. This was built for the Y.M.C.A. and its brown and buff Burmatoft terracotta façade mimics the style of the Y.M.C.A building in Brooklyn, New York that was built in 1885.

THE GREAT NORTHERN RAILWAY COMPANY'S GOODS WAREHOUSE
Built by the Great Northern Railway's architect A. Ross in 1897-9, this was one of the city's later railway constructions, but this combined goods station and warehouse revolutionised the storing and handling of goods distribution. It acted as a railway, road and canal interchange with the Manchester & Salford Junction Canal some 40 feet below accessed via shafts. It closed in 1954 and in the 1990s was used as a car park. Conversion to the leisure and retail complex seen today, which included the removal of the carriage ramp and viaduct serving the upper level goods station, was carried out in 1999-2000.

GREAT NORTHERN RAILWAY OFFICES

This long range of shops and offices was built at the same time as the warehouse and stretches the full length of Deansgate from Peter Street to Great Bridgewater Street, just across from the Beetham Tower. The buildings are only one room deep and formed a screen wall to the gargantuan goods station behind.

Inset: as seen from the 23rd floor of Beetham Tower

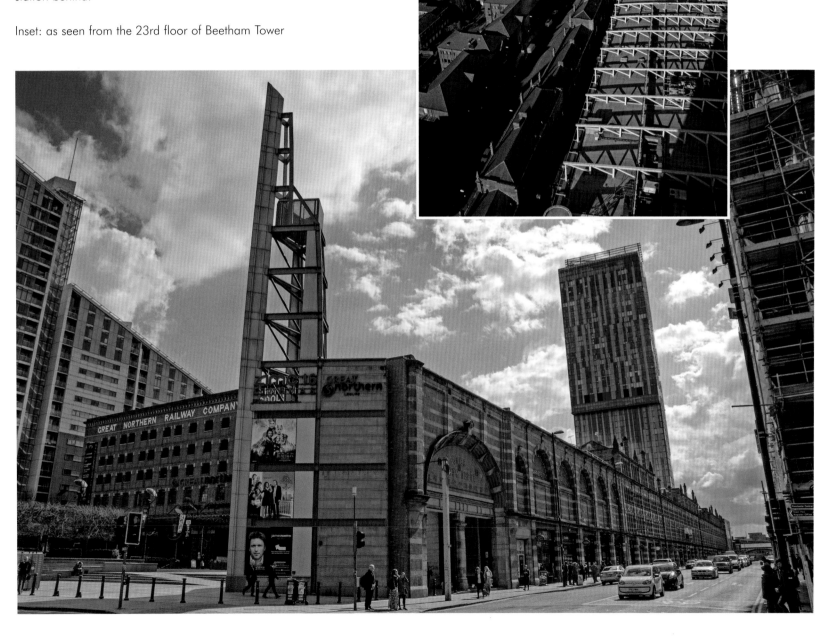

BEETHAM TOWER

At 48 floors high Beetham Tower is the tallest skyscraper in Manchester. The Hilton Hotel takes up the first 22 floors and levels 24 – 47 are residential 1 and 2 bed apartments. The building is topped with two penthouse apartments.

The twenty third floor is the location for the Cloud 23 bar from where, during the day, you can enjoy afternoon tea, with panoramic city views, from the comfort of an armchair.

SPINNINGFIELDS

This is the name given to an area of Manchester that is located between Deansgate and the River Irwell. Since 2000 it has been specially developed as a business, retail and residential area. The number of cranes visible in this view from the Cloud 23 bar clearly shows that development continues apace. This high-end retail hub is where many global companies have based their headquarters, exclusive boutiques have opened on its main shopping street, The Avenue, and hungry workers and shoppers have a choice of over 30 eateries.

MANCHESTER CIVIL JUSTICE CENTRE

Designed by the Australian architects Denton Corker Marshall and opened in October 2007 the Civil Justice Centre was voted one of Britain's ten best buildings by the highly respected architecture and design magazine *Blueprint*. This centrepiece of the Spinningfields Development area, nicknamed the 'open filing cabinet' for obvious reasons, is the largest civil and family court built in the UK in over 100 years.

By Spinningfields, new apartment blocks rise high on either side of the River Irwell. The bow-arched iron bridge on New Quay Street provides a link with the past with Manchester's Coat of Arms cast in iron at each end.

RIVER IRWELL

The River Irwell marks the boundary with the adjacent City of Salford. Two of the oldest bridges that link the two cities are Blackfriars (above) and Victoria (opposite). The three-arched sandstone Blackfriars Bridge, designed by Thomas Wright of Salford, dates from 1820 when it replaced a wooden footbridge built in 1761.

The single-arched Victoria Bridge's history is recorded on the northern battlement with the following inscription: 'This bridge was built at the expense of the inhabitants of the hundred of Salford, upon the site of the Salford Old Bridge of three gothic arches, erected in the year of our lord 1365. The first stone was laid in the first year of the reign of Queen Victoria, and the bridge was opened in the third year of her reign, and in the year of our Lord 1839, and was by Her Majesty's permission called Victoria Bridge.'

TRINITY BRIDGE

This three-way footbridge, located by Salford's Lowry Hotel, was designed by the Spanish architect Santiago Calatrava and was the first of a number of pedestrian crossings that are proposed to link the adjoining cities. From the Manchester side this single walkway forks in mid-air and curves left and right giving a choice of ramped pathways up and down the river on the Salford side. It was completed in 1995.

NEW BAILEY

The area on the opposite side of the river from Spinningfields is part of a Salford Central Regeneration Scheme to create a new business park offering Manchester 'a new business development within an established setting'. It takes its name from a prison that once stood in the area. The first office block 'One New Bailey' was due for completion in May 2016 to complement a Premier Inn hotel and striking 615 space multi-storey car park that has opened recently. The area is linked to Spinningfields via a second pedestrian footbridge lately placed in position.

SALFORD QUAYS

The city's vastly important trade link with Liverpool on the west coast was via the Manchester Docks and the Manchester Ship Canal that opened in the 1890s. Though not strictly a part of the city of Manchester, Salford Quays has been developed on the site of the docks, in what was one of the first urban regeneration projects in the United Kingdom following the docks' closure in 1982. Between 1986-90 the whole infrastructure of the area was modified. Roads, bridges and a promenade were built and an internal waterway network was created. Much residential development began, the Lowry Theatre (main photo) opened in 2000 followed, one year later, by the Lowry Outlet Mall, Manchester's only Factory Outlet Shopping Centre. Across the water the Imperial War Museum (bottom right), designed by Daniel Libeskind, opened in 2002 and more recently Media City, whose principal tenant is the BBC, was completed (bottom left).

On the promenade are a number of sculptures reflecting the area's industrial past. 'Casuals' erected in 2010 represents dock workers' union cards. These are arranged in two groups to reflect those that were in work and those that were left at the dock gates when the day's labour allocation had been completed. A number of former dockers were consulted for the project and some of their names and photographs feature on the 'cards'.

'Silent Cargoes' was designed by the artist James Wines. The varied assortment of barrels, packing cases, oil drums, sacks, chains and carts etc., all painted grey, portray the many activities associated with the neighbouring Trafford Park, which was arguably the world's first industrial estate.

CHRISTMAS

The festivities start with a spectacular firework display above the Town Hall which heralds the switching on of the street illuminations and the opening of the famous Christmas Markets.

The markets comprise over 300 stalls spread across around ten sites all over the city offering international food and drink and gifts, crafts, jewellery, clothes and toys from both European and local producers. A great time is had by all ages.

NEW YEAR'S EVE   The Manchester New Year is often, finance permitting, welcomed in with more fireworks. The 2013-14 event (below) was held in Piccadilly Gardens alongside the, now departed, ferris wheel. The 2015-16 pyrotechnics (opposite), which coincided with your author's retirement, were held by the Town Hall in Albert Square. The magnificent display was a fantastic way to celebrate both events!

Manchester – The Great City

ACKNOWLEDGEMENTS

In the preparation of this book I have travelled into the city many times. On each occasion I have been overwhelmed by the support and encouragement for this project received from many people. I was surprised to note that photography, subject to minor conditions, is allowed in many of the public buildings. Elsewhere, as necessary, I have sought permission to take photos within establishments and was not refused once.

I am eternally grateful and, in particular, would like to place on record my thanks for the assistance given by the following:

The management and staff at the Peveril of the Peak, The Palace Hotel, The Corn Exchange, Mr. Thomas's Chop House and Brown's Brassiere.

The stallholders at Afflecks.

The Librarian at the Portico Library.

The Station Supervisors at Manchester Piccadilly and Victoria Railway Stations.

The Hallé Venues and Events Manager.

Thank you all.